AFRICAN PRINTED TEXTILE DESIGNS

by Diane V. Horn

Stemmer
House
Publishers

Introduction

THE RICH AND VARIED WORLD OF PRINTED TEXTILE DESIGNS reveals the breadth and range of the aesthetic life in traditional Africa. This book illustrates designs that are printed, stamped or painted on the fibers; they do not reproduce woven patterns. In sub-Saharan Africa, the textiles with applied designs are made with few exceptions from vegetable fibers and fall into three classes: bark cloth, raffia palm and cotton. Bark cloth, a nonwoven textile, is made by beating the inner bark of certain bushes. Raffia palm is a non-spun fiber which can be woven, and cotton is a spun fiber. Beaten bark cloth may be painted and, at times, stamped designs appear on woven or imported cotton.

Nearly all of the prints illustrated in this book have been produced within the last century, because a combination of practical use and the effects of climate has deteriorated the fabrics, and some of the motifs have not resurfaced in more recent textiles. Though some of the designs are relatively new, each represents the traditional technique and artistry of an ethnic group or region. Many of the origins of the craft are obscure, yet almost all of them embody technical processes that are still in use and reflect contemporary African taste. An attempt has been made to illustrate what seems most exciting, either as overall patterns or as separate motifs.

Designs are created to decorate wraparound skirts, togas, shirts, shawls and headcloths, often fashioned from un-

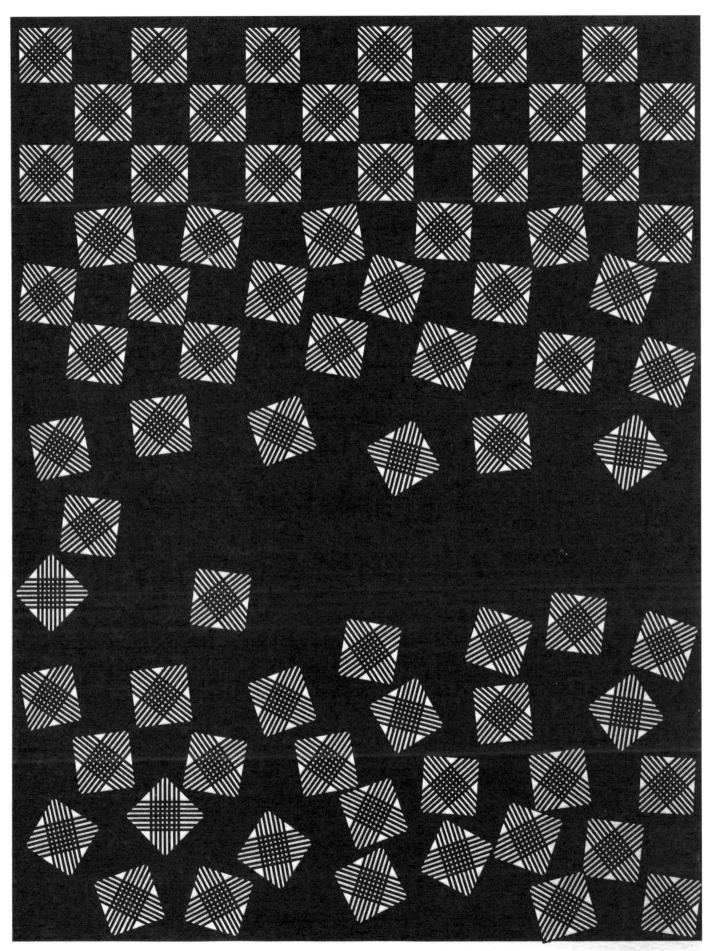

3

tailored rectangles worn by both men and women. Special types of designs adorn the costumes used in religious rituals and the costumes often include masks. Other designs are found on the apparel of hunters and warriors. African motifs are daily becoming more visible in the Western fashion industry. Many traditional designs may often be incorporated in clothing of all types, but the original cloths are among the most revered and prestigious of possessions in societies throughout Africa.

Because fashion does change, some aspects of the designs on clothing have disappeared and those that have persisted have become national dress. The culture that creates a textile pattern serves to document both continuity and change in aesthetic preferences, technology and social and religious traditions. Particular designs also serve as symbols of ethnic identity, wealth, prestige, status and the social roles of an individual.

Names of Patterns

The name given to each design or pattern often indicates the town where it is made or it may identify the ethnic group that produces it. All people who design textiles have, in their indigenous languages, descriptions of their process and their product. Frequently a verbal-visual link exists, in that a pattern represents a proverb, an event, an important object or creature or a mood. A few of these terms have become commonly used by producers and collectors and are presented here for convenience. The names of the patterns are followed by the ethnic group, the region and simplified design techniques.

This book is dedicated entirely to designs produced by methods other than weaving and embroidery. Some are common, such as adire, which is plentiful in West Africa, and adinkra of the Asante, the best-known stamped cloths. Also included are the lesser known bogolanfini, or mud cloth patterns, which are becoming ever more popular in the West.

Adinkra: Asante, Ghana

Adinkra, a rectangular, toga-size cloth, is decorated with stamped designs of symbols representing proverbs, historical events, persons or objects. The stamps are carved from calabash and applied repeatedly in rows. Thick black tar made from bark of the badie tree serves as the ink for the stamps. Adinkra, the name of the dye, means "good-bye," and the cloth was originally worn when guests were departing or during funeral ceremonies. In recent times, however, some of the designs carved on the stamps appear to be basically geometric and bear a visual resemblance to such objects as ladders, drums and combs, and are named accordingly. Traditionally, the black designs were stamped in squares drawn on black or rust colored cloth. More recently, they have also been stamped on white or brightly colored fabrics and used for decorative purposes. As many as 150 different designs may exist.

Adire: Yoruba, Nigeria

Adire cloth is a fabric with intricate white designs that stand out against blue indigo dye. Generally, starch, raffia or thread provides resistance to penetration of the dye. Lines are drawn that square off the cloth and then designs are placed within these boundaries. The designs are a combination of geometric lines, such as spirals, triangles, diagonals and dots, and shapes abstracted from natural forms, such as birds, flowers, snakes and fish. Two lengths, each 2 1/2 yards long by 1 yard wide, are designed with matching motifs and are sewn together to form the customary size for a woman's wrapper. The indigo-dyed fabric is patterned by several resist methods that are listed below.

Adire alabere: Tie-dyed fabric using thread as the resist. Thread is stitched into a pattern either by hand or with a sewing machine. In these fabrics, universally known by the tie-and-dyers as tritik, stitches may be drawn together tightly, so that the dye is prevented from penetrating the folds, or may be left flat, depending on the pattern desired.

Adire eleko: Fabric designed by hand-painting or stenciling with starch. Cassava or corn flour starch is either applied with a feather or brush in geometric designs or stylized animal or plant forms, arranged horizontally and vertically in rows of rectangles or squares, or forced through a metal stencil. The former method is employed by women; the latter is men's work.

After the starch dries, the cloth is carefully dyed, dried and scraped so that starch is removed. Hand-painted cloths are more finely detailed than are stenciled cloths, because hand-painting allows greater intricacy in execution. Hand-painting is also much slower than stenciling, but both types of adire eleko sell for approximately the same price in the market.

Adire oniko: Tie-dyed fabric on which the pattern is tied with raffia. Many pattern variations are possible. When the artist forms little peaks or clumps by tying alone or by tying seeds or small objects into it, the resulting fabric is called **onikan**. One common design variation, uniform rings arranged in a circular pattern, is called **eleso**. Folding the cloth into pleats which are bound with evenly spaced strands of raffia creates **olino**.

Gara: Any ethnic group, Sierra Leone

Any cloth dyed locally in Sierra Leone in natural indigo dye or in synthetic dyestuffs is called gara. The term originally referred to the leaves of a leguminous plant from northern Sierra Leone that yields indigo dye, but "gara" has developed a broader meaning, applying to all dyeing done as a small-scale industry. The majority of gara produced is tie-dyed through such methods as machine or hand sewing, or binding with cord into gathers or pleats. Sierra Leonean dyers are also known for resist-dyeing by dripping or stamping candle wax onto fabric, applying cassava starch in a pattern (see **kolingie**), or lifting areas of the fabric (bunching) and distributing dye on those areas to achieve a marbled effect.

Kolingie: Any ethnic group, Sierra Leone

Wavy or circular lines created by the starch resist method used in Sierra Leone (*see* **gara**), add subtle pattern to fabric. Kolingie means "comb" in Mandinka. Paste made from cassava or rice starch is spread on background fabric, favorites for which are satin and damask. A comb is drawn through the paste to produce a textural effect. The fabric is then dyed and dried before the starch is removed.

Korhogo cloth: Senufo, Ivory Coast

Black or dark brown stylized animal and human figures are painted on off-white, coarsely handwoven cotton cloth. Men execute the fine line drawings. The dark dye used is made of an aged mud solution. Motifs of geometric shapes and stylized human and animal figures, especially lizards, were painted in the direction of the warp threads on older cloths. Motifs of contemporary cloths have similar subject matter but appear in a randomized arrangement, placed crosswise rather than lengthwise. The zoomorphic figures had religious significance for secret societies, whose members wore the cloth for hunting or for dance. The designs seem to serve no traditional function today and the cloth is produced for purchase by foreigners.

Mud Cloth (bogolanfini): Bamana, Mali

Bogolanfini, a mud-dyed cloth of the Bamana people of Mali, is a living art form, constantly changing, reflecting new concerns, inspirations and patronage. Until recently, only women, and in particular Bamana women of noble descent, made bogolanfini. Traditional artists used techniques and motifs which, while expressing individual style and creativity, are based on well-known geometric patterns, and have been passed down through generations.

The complicated technique used for mud-dyed cloth has been known in the western Sudan for several centuries. Oral accounts state the origins of mud cloth lie in the Beledougou region of central Mali, an area which today is a center for mud cloth production and whose artists are praised for the skill and quality of their work.

The complex patterns of bogolanfini are produced on yellow-dyed, narrow-strip cotton cloth, by painting with river mud to form the dark areas. The yellow dye is then discharged from the remaining lighter areas, using a caustic solution. Numerous named designs and motifs are employed in patterning the cloth. For example, a recurring double linear pattern forming a number of squares is said to imitate the legs and body of the crocodile, and the double zig-zag motifs contained within these squares are known as "the legs of the cricket."

Conclusion

Hand-applied designs on African textiles are daily becoming more visible, not just in museums and galleries, but in the pages of magazines, in shop windows and on the streets of cities around the world. Adinkra patterns are appearing in Western countries on machine-made fabrics in the fashion industry, and adire cloth may often be seen incorporated into clothing of all types. However, the original cloths are among the most revered and prestigious of possessions in societies throughout Africa. Over the past century some of the designs have changed, but the quality has not been diminished. While some designs have vanished, others will take their place, as one might expect in a dynamic, resilient and adaptable African textile tradition.

D.V.H.

<h1 style="text-align:center">Illustrations</h1>

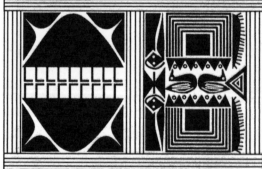
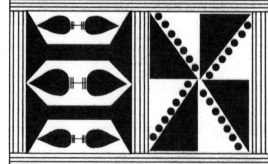

Bibliography

Aherne, Tavy D. *Nakunte Diarra: Bogolanfini Artist of the Beledougou.* Exhibition Catalog. Bloomington: Indiana University Art Museum, 1993

Mack, John and Spring, Christopher. *African Textiles.* Exhibition Catalog. Kyoto, Japan: The National Museum of Modern Art, 1991

Schuman, Jo Miles. *Art From Many Hands: Multicultural Art Projects.* Arts of West Africa. Worcester, Massachusetts: Davis Publications, Inc., 1981

Sieber, Roy. *African Textiles and Decorative Arts.* Exhibition Catalog. New York: The Museum of Modern Art, 1972

Wass, Betty and Murnane, Barbara. *African Textiles.* Elvehjem Art Center, Madison: University of Wisconsin, 1978

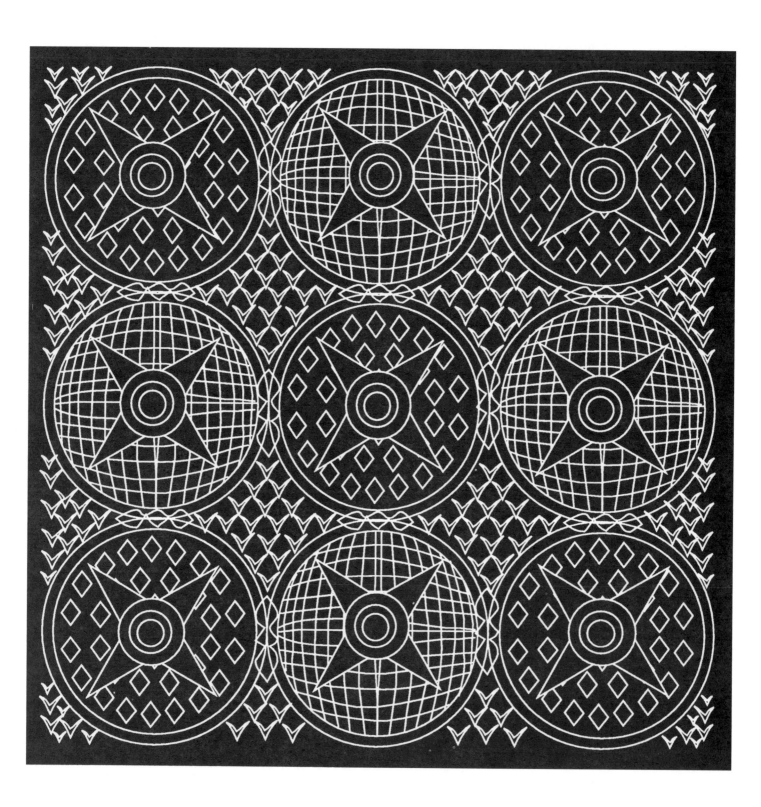

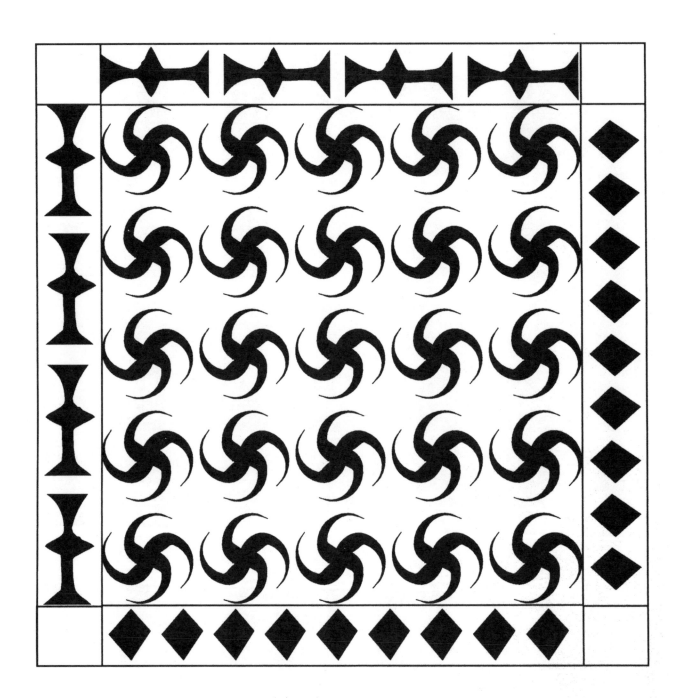

10

11

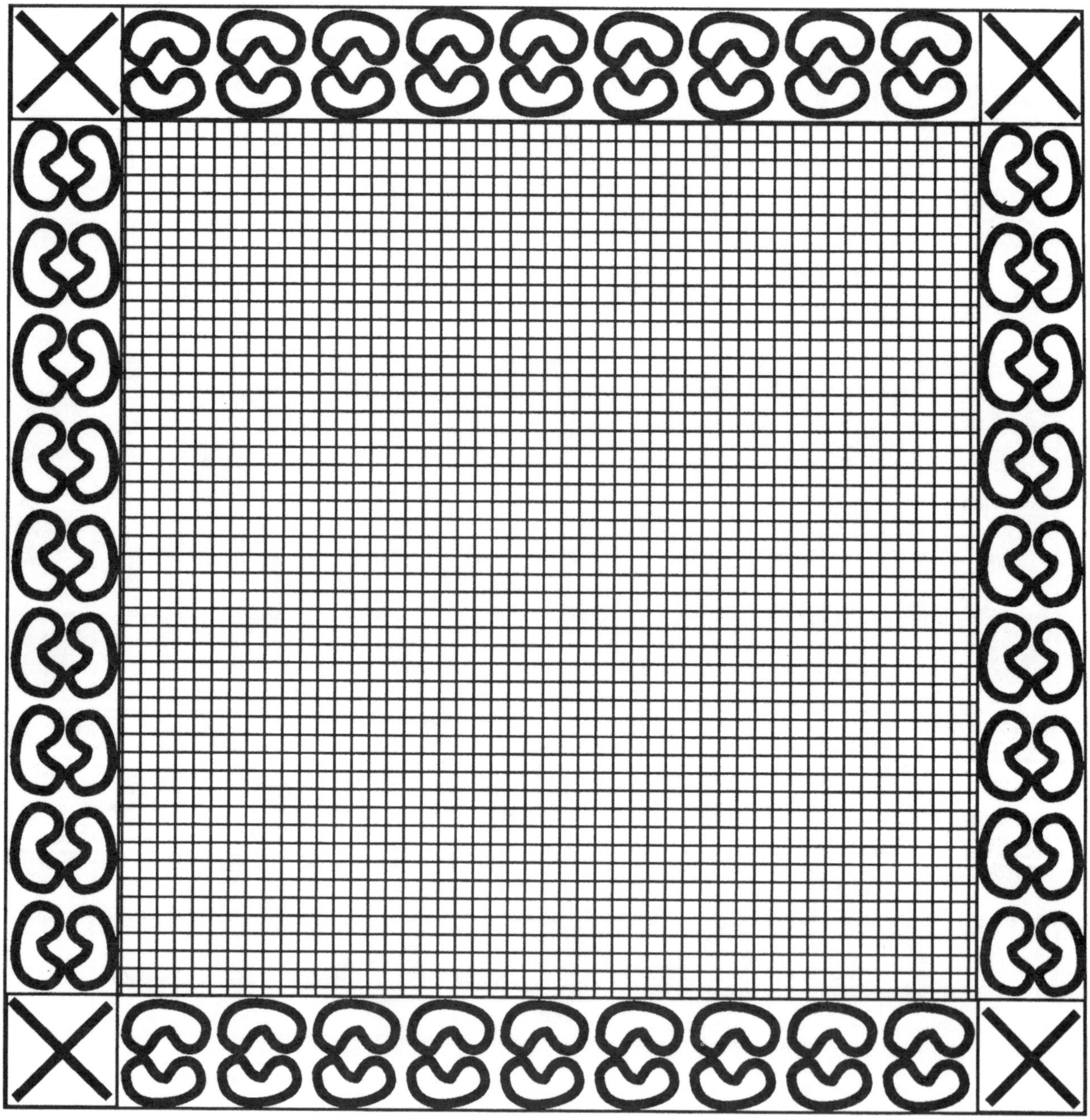

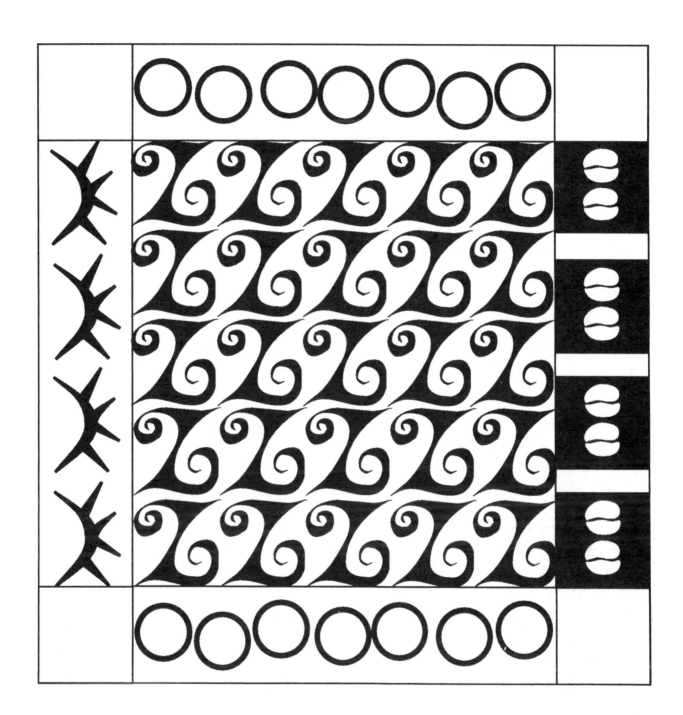

17

18

19

22

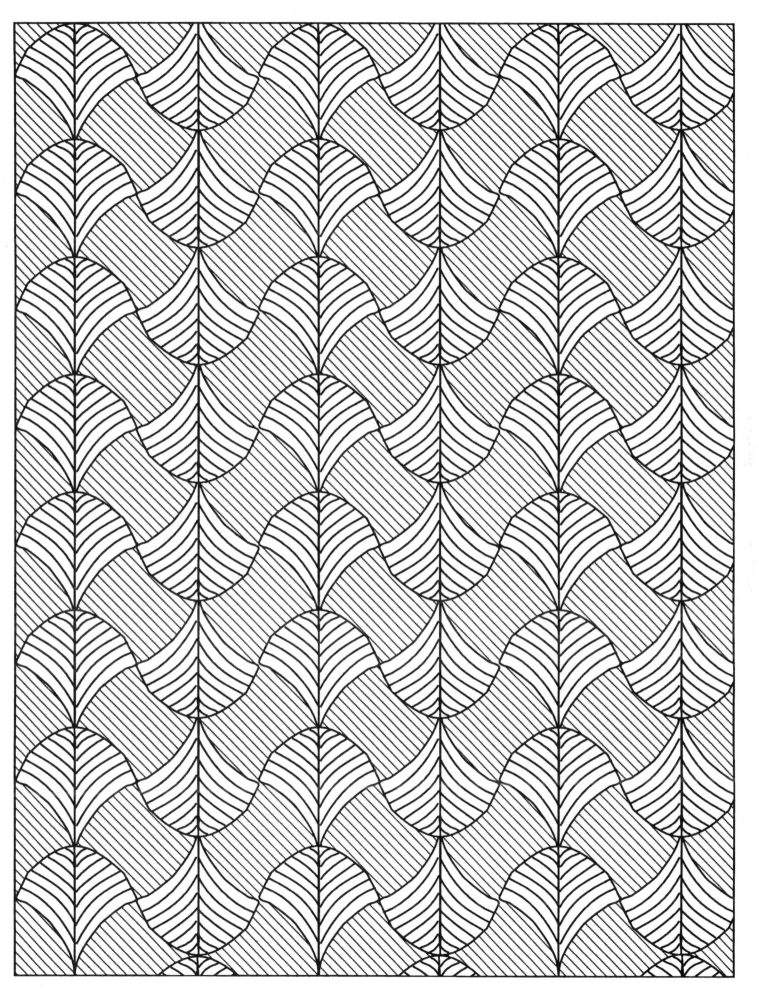

29

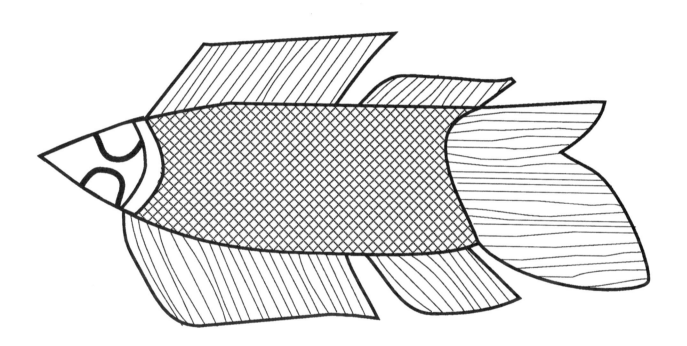

33

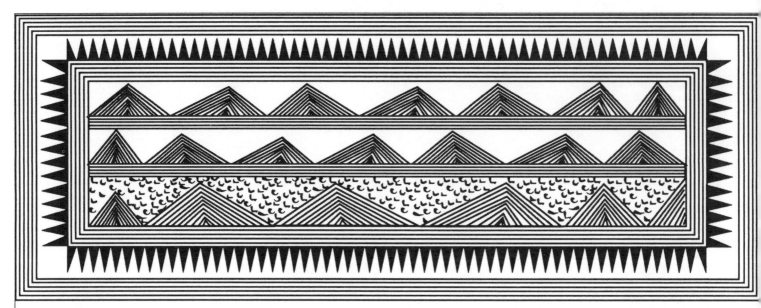

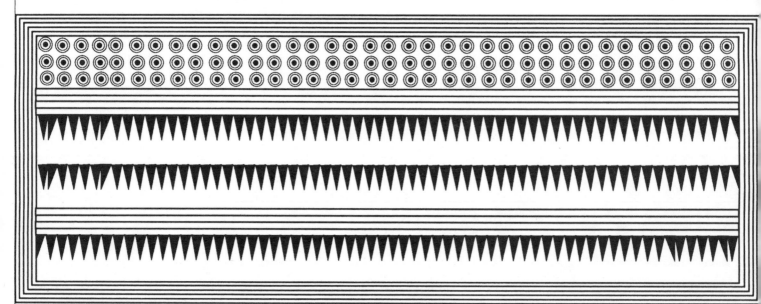

36

47

Colophon

48

Designed by Barbara Holdridge
Composed in Times Roman by Creative Computer Systems,
  Baltimore, Maryland
Color separations by Graphtec, Annapolis Junction, Maryland
Manufactured by Cushing-Malloy, Inc. Ann Arbor, MI